DEADLY BITERS

HYENAS BITE!

BY JANEY LEVY

Gareth Stevens
PUBLISHING

Please visit our website, www.garethstevens.com. For a free color catalog of all our high-quality books, call toll free 1-800-542-2595 or fax 1-877-542-2596.

Cataloging-in-Publication Data

Names: Levy, Janey.
Title: Hyenas bite! /Janey Levy.
Description: New York : Gareth Stevens Publishing, 2021. | Series: Deadly biters | Includes glossary and index.
Identifiers: ISBN 9781538257869 (pbk.) | ISBN 9781538257883 (library bound) | ISBN 9781538257876 (6 pack)
Subjects: LCSH: Hyenas--Juvenile literature.
Classification: LCC QL737.C24 L48 2021 | DDC 599.74'3--dc23

First Edition

Published in 2021 by
Gareth Stevens Publishing
111 East 14th Street, Suite 349
New York, NY 10003

Designer: Reann Nye
Editor: Meta Manchester

Photo credits: Cover, p. 1 Picture by Tambako the Jaguar/Moment/Getty Images; cover, pp. 1-24 (background) Reinhold Leitner/Shutterstock.com; p. 5 gualtiero boffi/Shutterstock.com; p. 7 pingebat/Shutterstock.com; p. 9 (spotted hyena) Jonas Stenqvist/500px Prime/Getty Images; p. 9 (Aardwolf) Joe McDonald/Shutterstock.com; p. 9 (striped hyena) Andrew M. Allport/Shutterstock.com; p. 9 (brown hyena) Marie Lemerle/Shutterstock.com; p. 10 Krakenimages.com/Shutterstock.com; p. 11 Sean Russell/Getty Images; p. 12 Marie Lemerle/Shutterstock.com; p. 13 Londolozi Images/Mint Images/Mint Images RF/Getty Images; p. 15 Niko Schoefer/Shutterstock.com; p. 16 Yatra/Shutterstock.com; p. 17 jacobeukman/iStock /Getty Images Plus/Getty Images; p. 19 Nomads Nature /500px/500px Prime/Getty Images; p. 21 Sir Francis Canker Photography/Moment/Getty Images.

Printed in the United States of America

Some of the images in this book illustrate individuals who are models. The depictions do not imply actual situations or events.

CPSIA compliance information: Batch #CS20GS: For further information contact Gareth Stevens, New York, New York at 1-800-542-2595.

Find us on

CONTENTS

Words in the glossary appear in **bold** type
the first time they are used in the text.

SAY HI TO HYENAS!

You may know hyenas (hy-EE-nuhz) from movies such as *The Lion King*. But real hyenas aren't anything like the ones you see in the movies.

Popular movies often show hyenas as bad guys and **scavengers** that aren't too smart. In truth, hyenas are one of Africa's most successful predators and are very smart. They have a powerful bite that is stronger than the bites of Africa's other great predators. Inside this book, you'll learn lots more about hyenas and their bite.

CHEW ON THIS!

You may know that **chimpanzees** are closely **related** to humans and are very smart. But a scientific study showed that hyenas are better at solving problems than chimpanzees!

Spotted hyenas, shown here, can live up to about 25 years and run as fast as 40 miles (64 km) per hour.

HYENAS' HOMES

If you want to see hyenas in the wild, you'll have to travel a long way from North America! They're found in many parts of Africa. Some kinds are also found in the Middle East and Asia.

One secret to hyenas' success is that they can **adapt** to almost any **habitat**. You can find them in grasslands, woodlands, along the edges of forests, in places that are almost deserts, and even high up in the mountains.

CHEW ON THIS!

Ancient hyenas first appeared in Europe or Asia—not Africa—about 1.4 million years ago. They were much larger than hyenas today.

WHERE HYENAS LIVE

MIDDLE
EAST

ASIA

AFRICA

■ HYENA TERRITORY

These are the areas of the world where
you can find hyenas in the wild.

WHO'S THE BIGGEST AND BADDEST HYENA?

Did you know there are actually four species, or kinds, of hyenas? Brown hyenas are the most uncommon kind. Striped hyenas have been studied the least. Aardwolves are the smallest and, unlike the others, only eat insects, small animals that often have wings and three body parts.

Spotted hyenas—also called laughing hyenas—are the largest species. They're also the ones most likely to be called **cowards** and bad guys. But that's not a fair account of this species. Let's take a closer look at these mighty predators.

CHEW ON THIS!

Spotted hyenas can be up to 4.6 feet (1.4 m) long and weigh up to 176 pounds (80 kg). Females are larger than males.

Spotted hyenas' ears are rounded, unlike the ears of the other hyena species.

STRIPED HYENA

BROWN HYENA

SPOTTED HYENA

AARDWOLF

9

THE ANIMAL'S ANATOMY

The spotted hyena is a strange-looking animal. Some might even say it's funny looking. It has a large head, big ears, strong **jaws**, and a long, thick neck. Its front legs are longer than its back legs, so that its back slopes down from front to back. Each paw has four toes with claws.

The animal's short, stiff fur is yellowish or grayish and spotted. A bushy tail and a short mane that sticks up along its back complete the look.

CHEW ON THIS!

People often think hyenas are some kind of wild dog. In fact, hyenas are more closely related to cats than to dogs!

Each spotted hyena has its own special set of spots.

CLAN LIFE

Spotted hyenas live in groups called clans. A clan may have up to 100 members. And a female is the clan leader! In fact, all females in the clan have higher **ranks** than all males in the clan.

Each female has her cubs in a private den. After a few weeks, she moves her cubs to a den shared with other cubs. Once males are grown up, they leave to join a new clan. But females stay with their clan for life.

CHEW ON THIS!

Cubs are born with dark fur. Their eyes are already open, and they already have some teeth!

Low-ranking males are forced to stay along the edges of the clan. But they can join in a hunt or a fight against another clan or other animals.

A BONE-CRUSHING BITE

Spotted hyenas have powerful jaws and special teeth that give them a very forceful bite. Their bite force has been measured at 1,100 pounds per square inch (77.3 kg per sq cm). That's more powerful than a lion or tiger's bite!

A bite force like that can smash bone. And hyenas don't only eat bone, they eat pretty much every part of their **prey**. They eat skin, hair, horns, and hooves. Most other predators don't even try to eat all those parts!

CHEW ON THIS!

Spotted hyenas can't completely **digest** hair, horns, and hooves. They throw up what they can't digest in little balls of matter.

The hyena is one of the only predators with jaws strong enough to tear through elephant hide and smash elephant bones.

TEETH

JAWS

HYENAS ON THE HUNT

Spotted hyenas may hunt alone or in groups. When they hunt alone, they hunt small prey. Their prey includes animals such as rabbits, foxes, porcupines, lizards, snakes, and fish. They also eat bugs and eggs.

They can hunt larger animals when they work in groups. Small groups hunt animals such as gazelles and impalas, two kinds of animals that are somewhat like deer. Large groups hunt animals such as zebras, buffaloes, **wildebeests,** and even rhinos and hippos!

CHEW ON THIS!

Studies have shown that spotted hyenas kill almost all of the food they eat. But they will scavenge if they have trouble finding prey to hunt.

Spotted hyenas can eat a lot at one time.
Their stomachs can hold 32 pounds (14.5 kg) of meat!

HUMANS AND HYENAS

Spotted hyenas are mighty predators, so you might wonder if they hunt people. In the past, hyena attacks on people were unusual. But they've become more common in recent years. Africa's human population has grown, and people are moving into areas where once only hyenas and other wild animals lived. This makes hyena attacks on people more likely.

But it's not just hyenas killing people. People also kill hyenas. People shoot or poison the hyenas in order to keep their livestock safe.

CHEW ON THIS!

In at least one part of Africa, hyenas moved closer to people after their prey left the area because there wasn't enough food and water.

Sometimes conditions in an area may produce a battle for survival between people and hyenas.

HYENAS IN DANGER

Officially, spotted hyenas aren't in danger of becoming **extinct**. Between 27,000 and 47,000 of them exist today. However, the number of spotted hyenas is going down, and some scientists are concerned about what will happen to them.

Aardwolves aren't in danger of becoming extinct either. However, striped and brown hyenas are in trouble. Their numbers are down and a major reason is that people are ruining their habitats. Don't let that happen! Hyenas are amazing animals that should be respected and kept safe.

CHEW ON THIS!

Hyenas are sometimes the prey of lions or leopards. But it's humans who put them in danger of becoming extinct by hunting them and destroying their habitat.

Hyenas have been misunderstood throughout history. You can help change that!

adapt: to change to suit conditions

chimpanzee: a smart animal that is a kind of ape and that lives mostly in trees in Africa

coward: someone who is easily scared

digest: to break down food inside the body so that the body can use it

extinct: no longer living

habitat: the natural place where an animal or plant lives

jaws: the bones that hold the teeth and make up the mouth

prey: an animal that is hunted by other animals for food

rank: a position in a group

related: two people or animals connected by family

scavenger: an animal that eats the remains of dead animals. To scavenge is to search for food to eat that's often already dead.

wildebeest: another word for a gnu, an antelope that looks a b like an ox with curved horns

FOR MORE INFORMATION

BOOKS

Duling, Kaitlyn. *Hyenas*. Minneapolis, MN: Bellwether Media, 2020.

Gagne, Tammy. *Hyenas: Built for the Hunt*. North Mankato, MN: Capstone Press, 2016.

Holmes, Porter. *Hyenas Stalk, Zebras Kick*. New York, NY: PowerKids Press, 2018.

WEBSITES

See Wild Dogs and Hyenas Face Off Over a Kill
www.nationalgeographic.com/animals/2018/09/hyena-versus-wild-dog-scavenging-video-animals/
Watch a video of hyenas and wild dogs fighting over prey killed by a wild dog here.

Spotted Hyena
www.onekindplanet.org/animal/spotted-hyena/
Discover some fascinating facts about spotted hyenas on this site.

Spotted Hyena Facts!
www.natgeokids.com/au/discover/animals/general-animals/spotted-hyena-facts/
Learn more about spotted hyenas and see some cool pictures on this website.

INDEX